INLAND

The True Story of a North Atlantic Humpback Whale

by

Lisa Capone

North Country Press

INLAND

Edited by Anne Nelson

Cover photo courtesy of The Whale Center of New England

ISBN : 978-0-945980-92-6

Library of Congress Control Number: 2011924641

Printed at Walch Printing, Portland, Maine

North Country Press

Unity, Maine

For my mother and my sisters, who introduced me to the sea.

~~L.C.

Foreword

Dan DenDanto's back yard was scattered with bones. Really big bones -- the bones of a humpback whale. Between piles of melting snow were graceful, curving ribs and chunky vertebrae, flipper bones that looked like huge fingers, and fragments chipped from a broad, sloping skull. Carefully, piece by piece, Dan studied

Photo courtesy of The Whale Center of New England

every bone and figured out where each one belonged. It was like putting together a giant puzzle.

Dan is a "rearticulator" -- a special kind of scientist who assembles skeletons of whales for museums and aquariums. On this late winter day in Maine, he was working on a very special animal -- a female humpback whale named "Inland" by scientists in Massachusetts, where she had lived. Soon, he would load all the parts of Inland's skeleton onto a truck and drive two hundred eighty-five miles south, from Bar Harbor on Maine's northern coast to The Whale Center of New England in Gloucester, Massachusetts. There, Dan planned to put the finishing touches on the skeleton with his friend Mason Weinrich, The Whale Center's chief scientist. Together, Dan and Mason would design the exhibit to fill a whole room at Mason's museum. They talked on the phone about Inland's skeleton many times while Dan worked on it in Maine. The two men decided just how they wanted the whale to look. With her tail held high, the young humpback would appear to be diving toward Gloucester's rocky shore. Dan smiled to himself. In a way, he thought, Inland was going home.

Table of Contents

SALEM'S BIG SURPRISE

People who live in Gloucester, Salem and other towns along the Massachusetts North Shore are used to seeing seagulls and crabs, and even harbor seals. But in the autumn of 2000, they got a gigantic surprise when a young humpback whale moved into Salem Harbor.

Gulls circled overhead, the sun sparkled, and seals poked their glistening heads above the calm surf as Kerry Griffin checked his lobster traps one cool fall morning. Rocked by gentle waves, Kerry's dinghy was the only boat out on the harbor that morning. It was peaceful and quiet -- just how Kerry liked it -- as he began pulling up a trap to see if a lobster was inside.

Then, suddenly -- Bffsshhh! Kerry was startled by a loud noise -- sort of like someone snorting. He turned around to find out

Photo courtesy of The Whale Center of New England

what made the strange noise, and almost dropped his lobster pot when he saw what it was. Right there, five feet away, an enormous bumpy black head broke the surface of the water. It was a humpback whale. Bffsshhh! It blew again, shooting water into the air through its blowhole. The whale was twice the length of Kerry's aluminum boat, and the lobsterman knew that, if it wanted to, the humpback could tip him right over into the ocean. But she didn't. The whale just watched him for a minute, looked at the lobster trap, and swam away -- leaving Kerry amazed. Kerry was no stranger to the ocean and its creatures. He grew up in Salem and lived near the city's waterfront his whole life, but this was a first. A whale in Salem Harbor! He could barely believe his eyes.

Kerry hurried to shore and started telling people about the whale. He told his three kids, and he called his friend, Mr. Gifford, the Salem Harbormaster.

"You'll never guess what I saw in the harbor," Kerry shouted into the phone. "A whale! It came up right beside my boat!"

Soon, Mr. Gifford saw the female humpback, too. She was hard to miss -- much bigger than anything Mr. Gifford had spotted

Photo courtesy of The Whale Center of New England

in the harbor before. Full-grown humpback whales can get up to fifty feet long and weigh forty tons. But, at two years old, this whale was already plenty big for Salem's small seaport. Her charcoal-gray body measured twenty-eight feet and she weighed about twenty tons. Sometimes the whale would raise her head and peek out above the water with big round black eyes. Other times, she dove, throwing her black and white tail up behind her. In the twenty-five years he had watched Salem Harbor, Mr. Gifford had never seen a whale this close to shore.

WHALE WATCHING

Mr. Gifford watched the whale all that day. Others did too. People walking along the shore and or relaxing on the green benches at Winter Island Park caught glimpses of it and told their friends and family. Salem's newspaper put the whale on the front page, and, the next day, more people arrived to see the city's humpback. Camera crews from Boston TV stations heard about the whale and wanted a closer look, so Mr. Gifford took the reporters and cameramen out in his boat. Soon, the whale was on the evening news. Then, hundreds of spectators came to Salem's breezy harbor front, wrapped in jackets and scarves, to watch the humpback that scientists called "Inland" -- because she liked to swim in near land, and because the underside of her tail (or flukes) displayed a black and white pattern that looked like the letters *I* and *L*.

Photo courtesy of The Whale Center of New England

It was easy to watch Inland. She often swam within one hundred yards of the coastline and was sometimes less than fifty feet from shore. Mr. Gifford said she got so close to boats in the harbor that people could have stepped right onto her back. Mr. Gifford patrolled the harbor in his boat every day, and every day he saw Inland. He watched as she swam out of the way of tanker

ships bringing coal to Salem's electric power plant, and as she
cruised past fishing boats and the lighthouse on Winter Island.

Inland stayed close by all fall. As trees dropped their leaves
and Christmas decorations went up, Inland wandered up and down

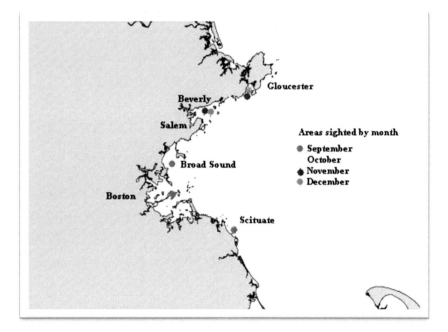

Map courtesy of The Whale Center of New England

the Massachusetts North Shore. She didn't always stay in Salem,
but she was never far away. Some days she swam a little north to

Gloucester Harbor, passing piers and lobster boats.   Sometimes she was just off the shore of Beverly, floating past beautiful seaside mansions. She liked Salem Harbor most of all, though, and people

Photo courtesy of The Whale Center of New England

"oohed" and "ahhed" to see her lunging through the water to catch herring and other small fish in her huge mouth. Humpback whales don't have teeth. Instead, their mouths contain hundreds of overlapping plates called baleen -- like a giant comb, made of keratin, the same substance human fingernails are made of. Inland gulped fish and saltwater all at once, then swallowed her food whole after squeezing the water out of her mouth through the baleen.

Sometimes Inland swam so near the shore that she floated in only ten feet of water. Mr. Gifford worried that she would get stuck at low tide. But she always seemed to know when to swim back out to deeper water where she was safe.

Inland stayed around Salem for so long that some people worried that she was lost or sick, but Mason at The Whale Center said she was a healthy whale. Mason watched Inland a lot, and he set up a computer web site where other watchers could write about their sightings. He said that, while it was odd to see a whale lunging for fish at the end of Salem's Pickering Wharf and swimming beside the city's power plant, Inland was doing what all humpback whales do in the fall. She was eating as much as she could, putting on a thick layer of fat before it was time to migrate south for the winter.

And, a few days after Christmas, that's exactly what she did.

A LONG JOURNEY BEGINS

Humpback whales are long distance travelers. One group of humpbacks migrates five thousand miles from the coast of Colombia, South America -- near the equator -- to Antarctica to feed, and then five thousand miles back again to Colombia to have their babies and breed. Inland was a North Atlantic Ocean humpback whale. She belonged to a population of about eleven thousand whales that breed and have their babies called "calves" in the Caribbean Sea near the Dominican Republic each winter. In summer, they come back to feeding grounds near New England, Canada, Greenland, Iceland and Norway. When they get there, humpbacks are hungry. The whales don't eat at all, not one fish, the whole time they are in the Caribbean.

When Inland left Salem Harbor on December 28, 2000, she knew where she was supposed to go -- partly by instinct and partly because she had made this journey before. When she was a calf, Inland and her mother swam north from the light blue waters of the Caribbean the first spring after she was born. Then, she traveled south again in the fall. Like other humpback calves,

Photo courtesy of The Whale Center of New England

Inland stayed with her mother for her first year, learning how to eat fish while she nursed on her mother's rich milk and gained up to sixty pounds a day.   The next year, she made the northbound trip again -- probably traveling, as many young humpbacks do, with a small group of two or three other whales.

But, this time, the two-year old whale migrated alone. Scientists like Mason keep in touch with each other, so he heard that Inland was spotted three days after she left Salem -- swimming through the Cape Cod Canal. People on Cape Cod knew it was Inland because of the markings on her tail. Humpback fluke markings are like snowflakes -- each one is different. Scientists take pictures of the flukes of each humpback they see and store them in computer programs that other scientists can check when they spot a new whale.

After that sighting on Cape Cod, though, Mason and other scientists in New England stopped getting reports about Inland, and they lost track of her. All through the winter, Mason, Mr. Gifford, Kerry Griffin, and all the folks who watched Inland swim and dive along the Massachusetts coast wondered about her. Mason knew Inland might not migrate all the way to the Caribbean this year. Since she wasn't yet old enough to have a baby, Inland might stop along the US coast near Virginia and Maryland, where some young humpbacks spend the winter resting and eating before heading up north again in spring. But, even if she traveled only that far south, Inland would still have to swim about six hundred miles. Everyone hoped she had eaten enough to keep her healthy for the trip.

NEWS FROM VIRGINIA BEACH

Months went by and spring arrived in Massachusetts. Snow melted and daffodils bloomed in Salem and Gloucester. And in April, just as Mason was preparing to welcome migrating whales back to New England, he opened his e-mail and got some bad news.

Halfway down the Atlantic Coast, Sue Barco, a scientist at the Virginia Aquarium, had received a phone call from someone who thought a whale might be caught in a fishing net about a quarter mile from shore. Sue specializes in helping to free whales and other animals that get tangled in nets. She quickly got a boat and went out to investigate, but it was too late. The young humpback whale had become tangled twice. One net twisted around its tail and then snagged on the anchor of a second net. Humpbacks can

Photo courtesy of The Virginia Aquarium

hold their breath underwater for about twenty minutes before they need to come up to breathe. Caught on the fishing net's anchor, this whale was trapped beneath the surface.

Sue had seen whales drown this way before. In fact, other humpbacks with scars caused by fishing gear had already died off the Virginia coast that same year. But, each time it happened, she felt sad. The Virginia Aquarium is called to help with about one

Photo courtesy of The Virginia Aquarium

hundred stranded marine mammals every year, including several whales. Sometimes, Sue's team finds out about the animals in time to save them. Other times, they aren't as lucky. Around the world, more than three hundred thousand whales and dolphins die in fishing nets each year.

Getting trapped in fishing nets is just one of many problems people have caused for humpbacks and other whales over hundreds of years. Whale hunters -- called "whalers" -- earn money selling products such as whale meat and oil. Before the invention of electric lights, people burned oil from humpback whales to light up house lamps and streetlights. Whalers in the 1800s and early 1900s killed so many humpbacks that the whales were close to becoming extinct. Finally, in 1966, it became illegal to hunt humpback whales. In 1986, laws protecting whales got stronger, when most countries around the world agreed to stop hunting not only humpbacks, but all large whales. The number of humpback whales has slowly increased, but they are still an endangered species. These days, pollution of their ocean habitat, and the risk of being hit by fast-moving ships or tangled up in fishing gear are among the biggest threats they face.

Off the coast of Virginia Beach that April afternoon, Sue and some helpers tied a rope to the dead whale and guided it to shore

Photo courtesy of The Virginia Aquarium

with their boat. They measured and examined the animal, and took pictures of it. They decided that the humpback was probably healthy before it got tangled in the fishing net. After the scientists finished their work, a man with a backhoe came and dug a hole over six feet deep in the sand to bury the whale. Meanwhile, Sue put the female humpback's pictures on her computer and e-mailed them to every whale expert she knew.

"Does anyone recognize this whale?" she asked.

Up in Gloucester, Mason clicked open the file that Sue sent, and he knew right away. There they were -- the black dots on a white tail forming the letters *I* and *L* -- flukes he had watched splash in and out of Salem Harbor all last fall. He frowned. Inland hadn't made it, after all. Mason was upset by the news. But, as sad as he was, he also knew what he had to do. He picked up the phone and punched in Sue's number.

"That's our whale," he said. "We need to get it back here."

BRINGING INLAND "HOME"

A whale turning up dead in a fishing net is never a good thing -- especially not for a scientist like Mason, who spends his life trying to learn more about whales and help them. Still, Mason thought Inland's bad luck might help save other members of her species. If The Whale Center in Gloucester could put Inland's skeleton on display in its visitors center, people would come and see it. The Whale Center could use the skeleton and Inland's story to teach tourists, families and school groups about whales and how to protect them from fishing gear and other man-made dangers.

"That whale lived here for quite a while last fall," Mason told Sue. "People remember her. Having Inland in our visitors center could help us save other whales."

"That's a great idea," Sue said. "How can I help?"

With Sue's help, Mason got permission from the U.S. government's National Marine Fisheries Service to take Inland's bones back to Massachusetts. In May 2001, a team from The Whale Center piled into a truck and rumbled off toward Virginia Beach. What lay ahead of them was a long and very smelly job.

Photo courtesy of The Whale Center of New England

After digging Inland out of the sand, the team used special "flensing" tools -- utensils invented by whale hunters -- to separate the whale's bones from the rest of its body. Then they loaded the skull and each bone into their truck and drove home to Massachusetts.

Photo courtesy of The Whale Center of New England

WHALE BONES

Back in Gloucester, Mason thought about how to put a whale skeleton together. Not many people know how to do it. Luckily, he knew two men who did. First, Mason called Tom French, a wildlife biologist who had worked on more than fifty whale skeletons before.

"What's the best way to clean whale bones?" Mason asked him.

Tom told him that the stinky job of working on a dead whale was about to get even messier.

"You need lots of horse manure," Tom said. "The bacteria in it will clean the bones and the heat will draw the oil out of them. Bury all the bones in manure."

Lisa Capone

Photos courtesy of The Whale Center of New England

So, Mason did. And, after five months in a steamy heap of horse droppings, the bones were ready for another one of Mason's friends -- Dan DenDanto, a biologist at the College of the Atlantic in Bar Harbor, Maine.

A guy who builds whale skeletons for a living is bound to have some unusual stuff hanging around, and Dan does. Fourteen huge steel tanks -- the biggest one measuring five feet deep and sixteen feet long -- sit in his backyard, like giant witch cauldrons. When the pieces of Inland's skeleton arrived, Dan put the big tubs to work. He filled them with water, added laundry detergent called Borax and then plunked in the bones. He heated the whole mixture almost to boiling. Whale bones are filled with oil, and

Photo courtesy of Dan DenDanto

heating them in water forces the oil to come out. It was like making a big whale bone soup.

After hours of simmering the bones, Dan used a mini backhoe to lift them out of the steel drums and into another homemade contraption: a plywood and steel pool, eight feet long by five feet wide and three feet deep. Dan filled the plastic-lined pool with a mixture of hydrogen peroxide powerful enough to eat through your clothes. The strong chemicals bleached Inland's bones to creamy white.

Finally, to keep Inland's skeleton clean, Dan coated the bones with a type of plastic called polyurethane. This helps keep the bones dirt-proof and makes them washable.

Now came the fun part -- putting the colossal skeleton together.

Dan had worked on lots of whale skeletons, but building

Photo courtesy of The Whale Center of New England

this one was trickier than most. Many of the bones were broken or

damaged when Inland was buried, and Dan had to fix them before

putting the skeleton together.

He got to work sorting the bones. The skeleton of a humpback whale weighs just under 1,000 pounds and is made up of 156 smooth bones that feel something like wood. Dan used sketches of other whales he had worked on to make sure he put each of Inland's bones in the right place.

For her spine, Dan strung fifty-five separate bones -- called vertebrae -- onto a steel pipe two inches thick and twenty feet long,

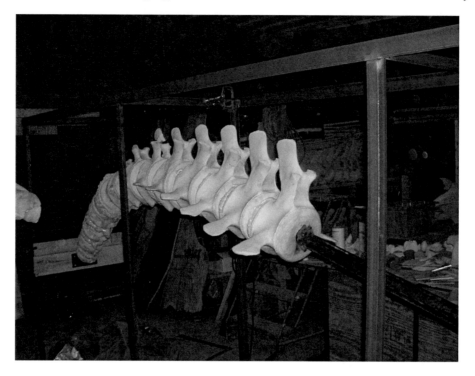

Photo courtesy of The Whale Center of New England

and put papier-mâché or putty between each bone. He and Mason had designed the shape of Inland's back so that the finished skeleton looked as if the whale was diving.

Then Dan put together Inland's flippers -- each one made up of twenty-seven bones. Building Inland's rib cage -- which, in life, collapses when a whale dives to keep the ribs from breaking -- would wait until the whole collection of bones was ready for final assembly in Gloucester. Her head would travel to Gloucester in pieces, too -- a huge sloping skull, two lower jaw bones, and lots of smaller bones in between.

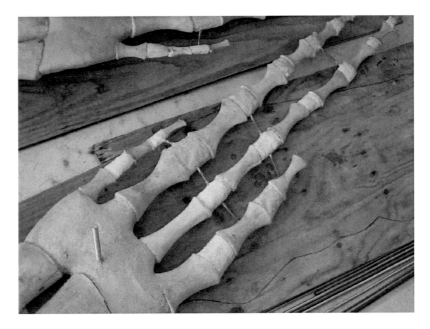

Photo courtesy of The Whale Center of New England

Dan and others noticed some unusual things while working on Inland's skeleton. Injured or strangely-formed bones in her neck and near her tail might have made it hard for the young whale to dive deeply, and easier for her to live near the coast in the shallower water of harbors and bays.

Dan built steel cages around each section of the skeleton, and then he put each section inside a plywood box. He stacked all of the cages and crates onto a twenty-four foot long flatbed trailer, and attached it to the back of his white pickup truck. Then Dan and some helpers headed south to The Whale Center of New England in Gloucester -- towing the skeleton of a well-loved, twenty-eight foot long humpback whale nearly three hundred miles in the pouring rain.

Photo courtesy of The Whale Center of New England

FINAL TOUCHES

Mason was excited when Dan and his crew arrived. Soon, Inland would have a new home close to the harbors she seemed to love while she was alive. Mason and others helped Dan carry Inland's skeleton into The Whale Center's building, piece by piece. First came the twenty-foot long spine, which was so big and heavy that

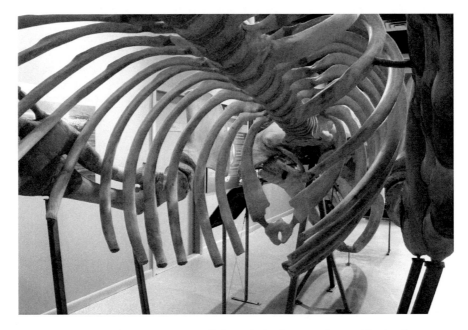

Photo courtesy of The Whale Center of New England

it took eight people to move it. Next came the skull and the lower jaw bones, twenty-eight ribs and, last of all, the flippers.

Photo courtesy of The Whale Center of New England

Dan had already spent three months preparing the skeleton. In the next two weeks, he attached Inland's rib cage to her spine using steel pins and glue, connected the sections of her skeleton together, and mounted the end of her tail bone to the back wall of Mason's visitors center. A local artist, who painted pictures of Inland when she was alive, painted her *I-* and *L*-marked flukes on the wall where the spine attached. Finally, more than two years after the project began, Inland's skeleton was complete. The exhibit could open to the public.

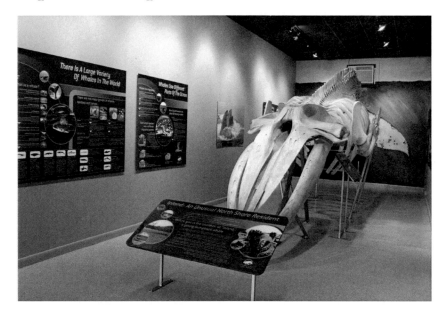

Photo courtesy of The Whale Center of New England

Conclusion

Inland's time for diving through the waves of the North Atlantic had been too short. Had she lived, Mason believes she would have given birth to many calves, helping her species to increase. Instead, Inland now has a different job to do. Her back arched and her tail held high, she helps Mason and other whale conservationists inspire people to care about whales, and to think of new ways of doing things so that fishermen, boaters, and whales can all share the sea.

Ten thousand people visit The Whale Center each year. Some of them remember the two-year-old female humpback that made a splash in Salem Harbor several years ago. Others are meeting

Inland for the first time. Small children look up at her huge skeleton, and grown-ups read her story on signs that hang around the exhibit. When they leave through a door that looks out onto the deep blue Atlantic Ocean, Mason hopes people carry a little bit of Inland with them in their hearts -- an appreciation for her life and the lives of all whales in every ocean around the world.

Glossary

Here are definitions for some words having to do with humpback whales and Inland's story.

baleen: Hair-like plates, made from keratin (the substance that makes up human hair and fingernails), which hang from the roof of the mouths of humpbacks and other whales that don't have teeth

biologist: A scientist who studies living animals and plants

blowhole: The opening through which a whale breathes

blubber: Layer of fat under the skin of most marine mammals, which keeps them warm

breaching: The behavior of a whale leaping out of the water and falling back in on its side or back with a big splash

bubblenet feeding: The cooperative way some humpback whales feed, by exhaling underwater to create a circle of bubbles that trap schools of fish

bull: An adult male whale

calf: A baby whale

cetaceans: Whales, porpoises, and dolphins

conservationist: A person who acts to protect wildlife and the environment

cow: An adult female whale

dorsal fin: The fin along the middle of a whale's back

endangered: A species or population of animals or plants in danger of becoming extinct

extinct: A species or population that is no longer living

filter feeding: The way baleen whales, such as humpbacks, strain their food from the water through baleen plates

flippers: A whale's front limbs or fins

flensing: A method used to remove the blubber layer from a dead whale

flukes: The two halves of a whale's tail

gulp feeding: A way whales feed by thrusting forward with open mouths to take in a large amount of fish and other prey

habitat: The natural home of an animal or plant

instinct: A natural pattern of behavior that animals are born with, such as a bird's instinct to build a nest in spring

lobtailing: The behavior of a whale slapping its flukes at the surface of the water

mammal: Warm-blooded animals that have hair and lungs, give birth to live offspring, and feed their babies with mother's milk

marine mammals: Mammals that live in the ocean, such as whales, dolphins, porpoises, seals, sea lions, walruses, manatees, and otters

Megaptera Novaeangliae: The scientific name for humpback whales, meaning "big-winged New Englander"

migration: The seasonal travels of whales to and from feeding areas, usually in colder seas, to warmer breeding and birthing grounds

prey: An animal that is hunted by another animal

rearticulation: The work of scientists who assemble animal skeletons

species: A group of similar animals capable of breeding with each other

spyhopping: The behavior of a whale that involves raising its head vertically out of the water, then sinking back into the water without causing a big splash

stranding: When whales and dolphins accidentally come onto shore

vertebrae: Bones that form an animal's backbone (spine)

whaling: The hunting and killing of whales for their meat, oil, baleen or other products

Resources

There are many groups around the world trying to help humpbacks and other species of whales. Here are some organizations to contact for more information about whales and how to protect them and their ocean habitat.

1. The Whale Center of New England, P.O. Box 159, Gloucester, MA, 01931, www.whalecenter.org

2. American Cetacean Society, P.O. Box 1391, San Pedro, CA, 90733, www.acsonline.org

3. Cetacean Society International, P.O. Box 953, Georgetown, CT, 06829, www.csiwhalesalive.org

4. International Fund for Animal Welfare, 411 Main St., P.O. Box 193, Yarmouthport, MA, 02675, www.ifaw.org

5. The Ocean Alliance & The Whale Conservation Institute, 191 Weston Rd., Lincoln, MA, 01773, www.oceanalliance.org

6. Pacific Whale Foundation, 300 Maalaea Rd., Suite 211, Wailuku, HI, 96793, www.pacificwhale.org

7. Whale and Dolphin Conservation Society, 70 East Falmouth Highway, E. Falmouth, MA, 02536, www.whales.org

8. WhaleNet (an educational website sponsored by Wheelock College) http://whale.wheelock.edu

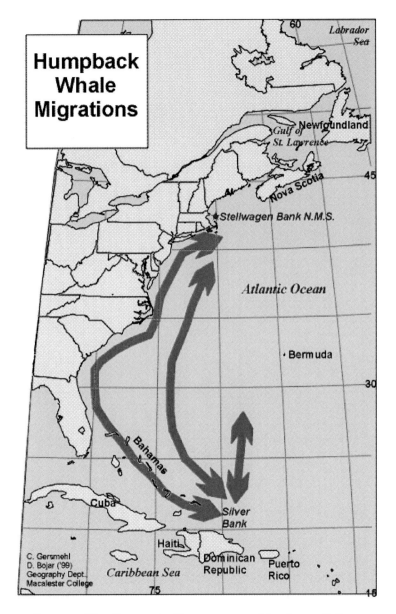

Courtesy The Geography Department at Macalester College

Deborah Bojar & Carol Gersmehl, mapmakers